I0836765

It's Lockdown 2021 in the midst of the relentless Covid19 pandemic. I'm innocently absorbed in a new Netflix show casually tuning out from the world. The theme song hits me like a wave of life.
It doesn't let go.

In the days to come, in my frantic search to buy and download this work of art, I discover it is hard to find - not yet officially released on Spotify or iTunes. My search couldn't end on that note and I carried on. To my surprise and delight, I found the voice itself, the musician. Clayton. And that is where this began. Pure and simple.

With truly inspired respect,
artist to artist.
London to Mumbai.

It's lockdown 2021. The world struggles to cope with the solitude and alienation that the global pandemic brought with it. This book is a humble reminder that kindness is, and will always remain, the most important language by which love is shared - transcending all limitations of geography, society and culture.

Worlds apart, this book began as an act of kindness shown by a stranger, giving shape and form to my words. With friendship gained it is our inspired creation ready to be shared.

May love and kindness be your portion today!

Humbled and grateful,
Dreamer to dreamer,
Bombay to London.

I love you like

the

Ocean

deeper than

is wide

I love you

like the fire

that burns me

hard into the

night

I love you like the tempest

Raging hard against my soul

I love you like the storm inside

I no longer control

I love you

like the rain

That's flooding streets

inside my heart

I love you like
the pain
of star crossed
lovers when

they part

I love you like the

Wind

that has ripped

my

sails

apart

I love you like

like it's

I love you
written
in the stars

I love you like the
stranger
who
will never

see your flaws

I love you
A

like the wager

I must win

when all is lost

I love you like

the knife

that cut through bone
and sinew
I love you like the scab
that is the only proof
of wound

I love you like
the tears

to which I've
cried myself to sleep

I love you
like the
somewhere
hidden 
deep I keep

fears

I love you like
the consequence
that I know
I must reap

I love you like
I love you
like no
one can

but me

I love you like the sailor
who left

home to tame the seas

I love you like the
writer naming things
you cannot see
I love you like
the soldier
who, bleeding,
by his

flag he stood

I love you like
the carpenter
carving beauty
out of wood

I love
you like
the painter
trying hard to
frame
the dawn

I love you like the
sinner
claiming he
was but a
pawn

I love you like the Saint

Who kept faith when all was gone

I love you like
like you

I love you
never ever saw

I love you like
the moment
which once
lived cannot
come back

I love you like
the stolen glimpse
that negates all
that is lack

I love you
like the souvenir
Thats worth more
than it's cost

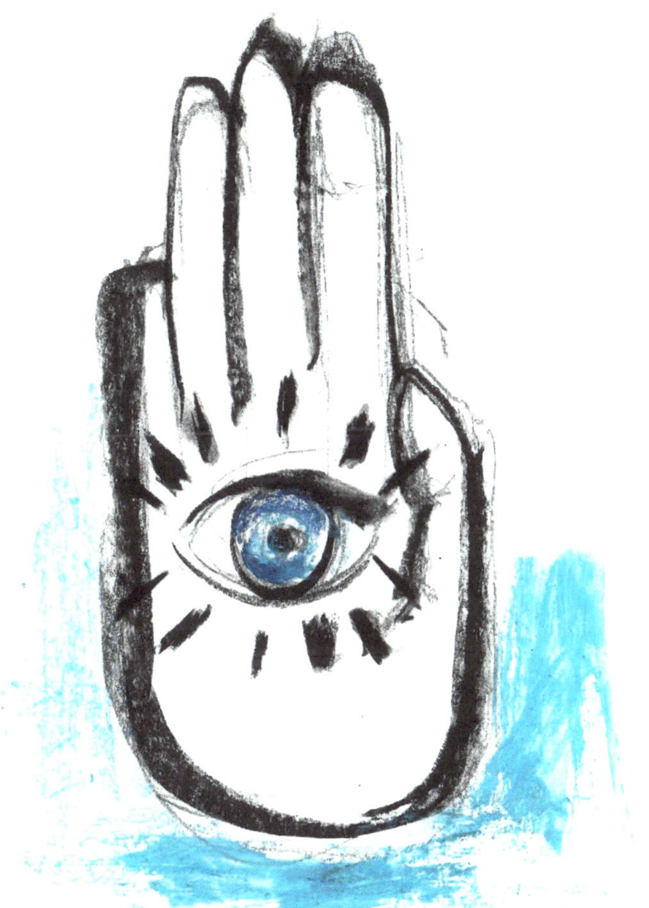

I love you like a memory
you once thought
was lost

I love you like
the failures

that haunt
me in my dreams

I love you like
the incompetence
in the mirror
that I see

I love you like
the incompetence
in the mirror
that I see

I love you like

the risk

that suffocates that

which could be

I love you like
I love you despite all
that is me

This is the first printed edition of **I Love You Like**, printed in England, 2021. Published by NISCHNASCH. **Written by Clayton Hogermeer, designed and illustrated by Natascha.** The author and illustrator assert the moral right to be identified as the creators of the work.

London, United Kingdom.
www.nischnasch.com
info@nischnasch.com
ISBN 978-1-912206-27-8

www.ingramcontent.com/pod-product-compliance
Lightning Source LLC
LaVergne TN
LVHW052309100826
845147LV00006B/710

* 9 7 8 1 9 1 2 2 0 6 2 7 8 *